Green
and Gold

D1420217

GREEN AND GOLD

THE WRENBOYS OF DINGLE

Steve MacDonogh

BRANDON

First published 1983
Brandon Book Publishers Ltd.
Dingle, Co. Kerry, Ireland

ISBN 0 86322 040 1 Hardback
      0 86322 041 X Paperback

Design: Brendan Foreman
Cover design and map: Syd Bluett
Typesetting: Leaders Phototypesetting, Swords, Ireland
Printed and bound in Ireland by Irish Elsevier Printers Limited, Shannon

Preface

I *hope that some day someone will write a fully researched book on the Wren, a task for which I have neither the scholarship nor the application. What I have tried to do in this short book is to combine photographs of the 1982 Wren with a short description of the preparations and the events of the day, some recent history of the Dingle Wrens as they are remembered here, and an indication of parallels with some other customs in the recent and more distant past. In considering the history of the hobby horse, the straw suits and other elements of the Wren and its origins, I have barely scratched the surface. I have also refrained from consulting large amounts of relevant material in the archives of the Department of Irish Folklore and in newspapers, journals and books. However, I hope that I have provided a basic portrait of this day of days in the Dingle calendar.*

I have spelt "Wren" thus throughout, though I have seen it spelt "Wran" in imitation of its pronunciation. I have also by and large used English-language terms, as — with the exception of the Gaeltacht Wren, An Dreoilín — these are the terms used by the participants in the Dingle Wrens.

Many people have helped in the writing of this book. My thanks go first and foremost to Fergus O'Flaherty, whose assistance was indispensable. He, like all the others who helped, is not responsible for the conclusions, which are my own, but he was wonderfully patient in the face of my constant badgering. My thanks go to Patrick Begley, Christine Bond, Breandán Breathnach, Leo Brosnan, Mary Jo Campbell, Frank Carroll, Dan Courtney, Paudie Curran, Brendan and Grace Daniels, John Farrell, Anton Flannery, Jimmy Flannery, Kathleen Flannery, Alan Gailey, John Joe Gleeson, Bernard Goggin, Michael Graham, Dinny Joe Griffin, "Sergeant" Houlihan, Tom Long, Tom Lynch, James McKenna, Venetia Newall, Séamus Ó Catháin, Aodán Ó Conchuir, Bairbre Ó Floinn, Ríonach Uí Ógáin, Kevin O'Sullivan, Maurice Rohan, John Joe Sheehy.

Dingle in mid-Winter

Introduction

Thrusting into the Atlantic ocean at the extreme western edge of the "Old World" of Europe, the Dingle peninsula enjoys mild winters, with little frost and only occasional snow which rarely settles except on hill and mountain tops. But gales are common and sharp squalls carry fusillades of hail and sudden rain or sleet. Bright days are few and grey clouds shift rapidly in endless succession behind winds from the west.

It is a dour, desultory season. Pool tables, removed in the summer to make space for tourist customers, return to pubs. The town huddles with a grey cloak about it against the lack of light and warmth; damp enters houses and bones with more effect than dry cold. This is the dull and unproductive season for agriculture and tourism. The parade and bustle of brightly dressed visitors, bringing the languages of France, Germany and Holland, the accents of America, Australia and England, has ended in October, and the restaurants are closed. On the farms there is always work to be done but winter's grudging routine impells frustration and inertia more than energetic husbandry.

The Christmas season sees a festival not only of the community that lives and works in Dingle but also of those who, born and brought up in the area, live and work or study elsewhere. At Christmas the population is suddenly multiplied by the arrival home of the sons and daughters of the place from Dublin, Cork, Limerick; from almost every county of Ireland. The pubs are suddenly fuller, resounding to the animated exchange of news and renewal of friendships. St Patrick's Day, Easter and other holidays also see these exiles returning for visits. Indeed, many of the young people drawn to cities travel home for very many weekends throughout the year, despite journeys of up to eight hours each way. But Christmas is the largest gathering, and in Dingle it takes on a particular festive form on St Stephen's Day, the day of the Wren.

The Wren is an explosion of light, colour and boisterous exuberance in the midst of winter's gloom. From damp, cold lifelessness the town erupts into a day's release in marching, music, shouting, dance, fooling and drinking. Many of the characteristics of the Wren originate from early, even pre-Christian sources, but the festival is not a quaint revival of ancient custom or pagan religious ritual. It is a living thing which survives because it serves a function: it is a way that people find to enjoy themselves.

Christmas as it is celebrated in the Western world is a relatively modern festival, but people have always found the end of the old year and the beginning of the new, the heart of dark winter, an appropriate time for celebration or festival, for summoning the spirit of anticipated spring.

Festivals such as the Wren took place all over Europe from at least as early as the first century A.D. In the Graeco-Roman world the Kalends of January were celebrated during the twelve days around 1 January by men disguised with beards, or as women or as animals, who engaged in wild orgies, even to the extent of human sacrifice. Timothy, the first Bishop of Ephesus and a correspondent with St Paul, was sacrificed at such a festival. For all its violent character, this was a celebration of the old religion, and the Church issued many denunciations of its continuance over many centuries. Particular condemnation was reserved for the custom of wearing animal masks, which were seen as representing demons released from the underworld.

Yet the festival in various forms survived all the efforts of the Church. As Margaret Dean-Smith concludes in her introduction to Violet Alford's *The Hobby Horse and Other Animal Masks*:

> . . . all over Europe, even in Britain, there are local survivals of such festivals and such disguising to the present day, pursued with a purpose, and with regard to propriety of season which however vaguely understood, or formulated by the participants, removes them from mere boisterous and uninhibited jollification, or "play" in the sense of voluntary activity. They are compulsive, purposive acts; and their purpose, however manifested in buffoonery, is the increase of virility in man and fertility in cattle and crops. [1]

This view of local festivals and customs such as the Wren regards them as survivals of pagan religious practices, but this should not be taken to imply that there is any consciousness of their origins amongst present-day participants, nor that their modern function has anything in common with their earlier pagan dedication and function. As Venetia Newall writes in relation to English Fire Festivals:

> A vital feature of participation in, and therefore survival of, these festivals, is the fact that they are regarded as great fun, and hence a means of releasing tensions. On the other hand, no conscious link can be traced with past notions of fertility ritual or similar rites. The participants certainly appreciate the historical factor, the point that they are doing what previous generations did before them, but this is productive of a sense of continuity, not of pseudo-religious awe. There is no impression that, should the festival lapse or fail in some way or other, any supernatural calamity will overtake the community. [2]

Until quite recent times the Wrenboys were a feature of the Christmas season in most parts of Ireland, although in some places — particularly in the province of Ulster and in County Wexford where strong Scottish and English influences intervened — the similar custom of mumming prevailed. A broad range of the provincial newspapers in December 1940 and January 1941 included items on the Wrenboys: there were reports from Cavan, Dundalk, Enniscorthy, Kerry, Leitrim, Limerick, Longford, Mayo, Carlow, Clonmel, Roscommon, Sligo, Westmeath and Wexford, most of which remarked upon the decline of the custom. To the present day, children tour houses collecting money on St Stephen's Day in many parts of the country, and in Listowel, County Kerry, a revived version of the Wren sees an annual All-Ireland Wren Competition take place in September.

What is unique about the Wren in Dingle is that it has continued as an unbroken tradition, undergoing changes with the years, but never dying out or being changed in the way associated with conscious revivals. It is clear from oral and written sources that the present-day Dingle festival is directly descended from the Wren customs of the last century; but as to how far back the tradition extends it is impossible to know.

Dingle

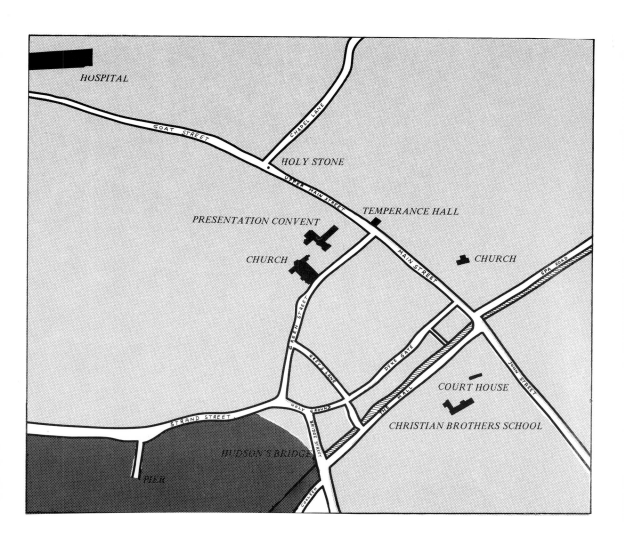

Green and Gold

Green and gold: green, the colour of grass, of growth, the colour of spring, of fertile land; the green fields of Ireland, the emerald isle. Gold for the sun — sickly, misted or absent during winter, welcomed in spring — and gold for ripened crops and straw.

Green: St Patrick's colour. Gold: St George's. Green and gold: the colours, almost, of the flag of the Republic. Green and gold: the colours of Kerry and its glorious football teams. Green and gold: the colours, too, of the Wren in Dingle which draws its support from Green Street, Dykegate Lane, Holy Ground, Bridge Street and the Mall.

The first step towards the Green and Gold Wren of 1982 was taken on Tuesday 14 December with a meeting in Paddy Bawn Brosnan's pub in Strand Street. Ten people attended the meeting which was chaired by Fergus O'Flaherty of O'Flaherty's pub in Bridge Street, prime organiser of the Green and Gold. For many months Fergus had been speaking regretfully of declining support for the work of organising and preparing for the Wren.

"It is going down definitely," he said, despite the fact that more had marched on the previous year's Wren than anyone could remember. It seemed like a protestation designed to provoke others to become involved in organising.

Fergus O'Flaherty's family was one of many moved into the town by Lord Ventry in the 1880s from Rinn Bheag, which faces Dingle across the harbour. Both his mother and father were musicians, and Fergus and Mary Mazzarello, his sister who runs a record shop in Green Street, maintain the musical tradition in the family. Fergus is an energetic organiser and is chairman of Craobh an Aghasaigh, the Dingle branch of Comhaltas Ceoltóirí Éireann, the national organisation for traditional music. Musicians from Craobh an Aghasaigh, under the name of Slaudeen, issued a record in 1983 entitled, "Forever by Dingle Shore". Fergus has also edited and published a local magazine, *An Ridire*.

Fergus O'Flaherty

Now in his thirties, Fergus has been organising the Green and Gold since 1968, but most of those at the planning meeting were in their early twenties. Peter O'Regan works in the Dingle boatyard where his father was foreman. Noel (Purdge) Murphy, tall, with a shock of dark curly hair, and cigar-smoking, is a popular local character who hails from Ballydavid in the west of the peninsula and lives now in Dingle where he works for Posts and Telegraphs. Louis Graham, like his father, is a fisherman; and Tony O'Connor, whose father was a taximan and ambulance driver, delivers and drives for Ashe's, local agents for Guinness. Liam Long is a farmer and fisherman.

It was John Greaney's first year of involvement in the Wren; trained as a pilot at nearby Farranfore, he works in the family grocery shop in Green Street and restaurant in Holy Ground. His father, also John, established an organisation for the care of old people in Dingle, and it is in the homes in the Mall that Kathleen Roche, from Birmingham and the only woman at the meeting, works. John Murphy, short and white-haired, is in his forties and is another newcomer to Dingle, working in a small fibreglass plant in Milltown. Ciaran Cleary, at fifty the senior member of the party, was a fitter in Newbridge, County Kildare, and in England, who returned to his home town of Dingle in the 1970s. And a latecomer to the meeting was Eamonn Farrell of the Corner House guesthouse in Dykegate Lane, who works with Posts and Telegraphs.

Planning meeting of the Green and Gold: (left to right)
John Murphy, Noel Murphy, Ciaran Cleary, Peter O'Regan
Louis Graham, Fergus O'Flaherty, Liam Long, Tony O'Connor,
John Greaney, Kathleen Roche

At the meeting, after tribute had been paid to Tommy Barry, organiser of the Wren for many years who had died earlier in the year, the first subject discussed was oats; sixteen sheaves would be needed by Monday for the making of eight straw suits. The next Tuesday was agreed as the night for making the straws, and Ciaran Cleary offered his premises. Kathleen Roche was jovially advised not to sit on a gas heater if she were wearing a straw suit. Peter O'Regan volunteered to repaint the banner poles. The head of the hobby horse was also in need of painting and another volunteer readily presented himself. There was some discussion of the advisability of making a new horse.

"We could make a new head for it, we could make a new horse altogether."

"The head's alright; you can't change the traditional hobby horse's head anyway."

"There was one year we had corns out of its ears."

"We should leave the head alone anyway."

"If you extend it back a bit you could have two people under it and it would have four legs under it."

"Would that be breaking with tradition?"

"No. I don't know. It'd look better with four legs."

It seemed unlikely, however, that anyone would have the time or the inclination to build a larger frame for the hobby horse.

The organisers of the Green and Gold annually take the responsibility of providing a Christmas tree beside the bridge near O'Flaherty's. Various people agreed to check the tree lights for faults, to dig a hole for it, to bring it in with tractor and trailer and set it up.

"This year we'll be getting the tree legal," said Fergus, "though I'm not saying it wasn't above board before."

The previous year the Green and Gold had featured a float, of the kind well known to parades elsewhere. It was generally felt to have been an impressive addition, showing a particular seriousness. "It's spectacular, it's something else," was an opinion agreed with by all. Proposals were voiced for the theme of the float; "a mockery of Sally O'Brien", "something about the Ranga", "E.T., you know, the star of the film" were foremost among the suggestions. The mention of

Sally O'Brien, fictional character in a lager ad who had become a household name, evoked a few groans and laughs. A final decision was postponed, but volunteers agreed to check on the availability of a float and collect it from Tralee.

Fifes had been gathered from the houses they had scattered to following the previous Wren. Drums were to be brought out and warmed; one drum was to be painted with the Green and Gold legend.

Several different options were proposed for the order of the march; all seemed agreed that the hobby horse and banner should head the procession, but it was unclear whether the float should follow or precede the musicians. It was felt that the eight strawmen should be together.

Little discussion of the route was required beyond deciding whether a visit would be paid to the hospital.

"Definitely, we should go in."

"Just go in around the wards and no collecting."

"Oh, no collecting, definitely."

"It's a good gesture."

"Will we get in?"

"We were left in last year."

"But we didn't get in three years before that."

"There'll be no drink the first round, and we'll go in then."

There was no controversy over the destination of the money collected during the Wren: Beaufort Hospital, as in the previous year. There was, however, some concern about the fact that the Wrens from outside Dingle might collect in Dingle a day earlier. With St Stephen's Day falling on a Sunday, the tradition was that Dingle town Wrens would take place on the Monday, not wishing to be limited by the shorter pub opening times on Sunday; but the "country" Wrens would be on the Sunday. The Green and Gold and other Dingle groups could find themselves at a disadvantage in collecting. However, there was nothing they could do about it.

The meeting had got through its business smoothly and efficiently. There had been a level of agreement, of shared experience and conceptions which had meant there was no real need for debate. Responsibilities had been easily apportioned and it only remained to be seen whether they would be acted on as readily as they had been accepted. The mood of the meeting relaxed, only gathering about it an aura of officiousness as the minutes were read by Noel (Purdge) Murphy while Tony O'Connor recorded the moment on video, for the benefit of whose audience beer glasses were removed from tables.

After all his forebodings, Fergus was pleased with the meeting and it was with some affection that he said, "You're all mad to be involved in this," and with satisfaction that he said, "It's the preparation that makes the day."

One week after the first meeting there was a gathering in the evening at O'Flaherty's pub where drums stood before a gas heater and fifes lay on the bar counter coated with olive oil. The physical appearance of the pub has a highly individual, even bizarre charm. Miscellaneous bric-a-brac lines shelves on three of the four walls. Old advertisements for P&O liners, drums, ancient radios, paintings, "Buy Irish" and drink ads jostle with trays, large letters spelling "Fáilte," and pictures of Kerry football teams. Below the shelves a motley collection of posters, photographs, tea towels bearing various designs, songs, postcards and drawings adorn the walls. The floor is made of large stone paving flags. In the corners of the ceiling which is supported by two slender wooden poles are painted two harps and two large green shamrocks. Until recently the bar counter was a low affair covered with tarpaulin, and seating was provided by beer barrels. After time for a few pints there was a general move down the street to Ciaran Cleary's where the accoutrements of the Wren were laid out. The two rooms had been used as election offices during the preceding general election: posters and leaflets lay scattered about the floor and the face of Charles Haughey, leader of Fianna Fáil, cast its gaze from almost every corner.

Much had been done in the intervening days: the tree had been acquired, erected and dressed with lights which had been connected by the ESB; green and yellow paint had been bought; Purdge had brought into town oats from his family's farm in Ballydavid.

John Murphy brings oats into Ciaran Cleary's

The oats were carried in from a yard nearby; twine was stretched across the room and to this were tied bunches of four or five long golden straws. Each succeeding bunch was tied over the loose end of the preceding knot, so tying all together until a length of some 40 inches was achieved and the twine was then cut. Each length constituted one third of a suit — the skirt, top or headdress. Then twine was stretched again and more lengths made.

Making straws, 21 December

☆　　☆　　☆　　☆　　☆　　☆

In the past, the strawboys were most commonly associated with weddings. Young men of the neighbourhood, disguised in their straw suits, would go to the house where a wedding party was in progress, and their Captain would demand a dance with the bride. Memories of the custom are dim in Dingle, but Paudie Curran suggests that they were not particularly welcome guests.

"They were only going there for trouble. They'd ask for drink, but they wouldn't be left in the house; they might get drink brought to them outside. If they got no drink, they'd start making trouble, maybe firing stones at the house; and if they got drink, too, they'd make trouble, because of the drink they had taken." This was a custom of the countryside around Dingle and of rural areas all over Ireland; and Paudie Curran vaguely recalls conflict between rival groups of strawboys and even, on one occasion, the kidnapping by strawboys of a woman of one parish to secure her marriage to a young man of their own parish.

In other parts of Ireland strawboys sallied out on All Hallow's Eve and engaged in minor vandalism at the homes of unmarried women. Treading a delicate line between high-spirited pranks and downright harassment, they would steal food, compel women to dance or generally make nuisances of themselves.

Trying on a suit

The role of the strawboys in the Dingle Wren is different. Much of the pleasure of the occasion is in making the straw suits, and on the day itself they take part in the general parade and collect money. The same would have been true of the strawboys who took part in mumming in Ulster and in Wexford. Of course, the element of disguise afforded by the straw costumes is important and offers opportunities for them to grab women and girls in ways that would not be attempted on any other day of the year.

At "Up-Helly Aa", the pageant which takes place at the end of the Christmas holiday in Lerwick, the capital and main port of the Shetland Islands, those who wear costumes are known as "guizers" (as in dis-guise), and

> The oldest guizing costume was made of straw and those who wore it were known as the Skeklers. A squad of these local straw-boys appeared in 1977 . . . "It was the traditional guizing outfit," remembers Tom Anderson. "In the old days you made your own straw suit. They were called Grulicks on Unst (one of the Shetland Islands): Black Grulicks and White Grulicks. The Black Grulicks wore black material and burst in, so they were called Raiders. The White Grulicks wore straw and came in dancing and invited the ladies to dance. It goes back hundreds of years: they did it for weddings." [3]

Earlier references to the Shetlands strawboys are found in *Rambles in the Far North* by R. Menzies Fergusson (2nd edn. 1884), and in a January 1878 report in *John O'Groat's Journal*: at Old Style Christmas "there were some of them dressed in straw and they attracted their full share of attention, and in a few of the aristocratic families received a hearty welcome." [4]

In eighteenth-century Ireland the Whiteboys, in carrying out a violent campaign against the consequences of an extremely oppressive system of land holding, adopted the dress of the strawboys. While the straw suits offered the practical advantage of disguise, they were also a strong element in the folk customs of the rural poor; they constituted a symbol of community which was entirely appropriate to the collective action against unjust rents and tithes.

But the straw suits are by no means confined to Ireland and Britain. Their occurrence in Portugal and Spain has led to their being ascribed a Lusitanian or Galician origin. [5]

Recalling the Dingle Wrens of his youth in the 1920s, Michael Graham of Gray's Lane says with a mischievous smile: "Nobody could wear straws only a qualified drunkard, and he was a terrifying apparition!"

☆　　☆　　☆　　☆　　☆　　☆

Making straws, 21 December

As people got into the swing of the preparations, most worked to make the straw suits, while Peter O'Regan stripped loose paint from the banner poles and painted them afresh in the green and gold colours. The lengths of straw ready to be made into skirt, top or headdress were piled up beside the door as they were finished. Fergus, with help from Purdge, set to work on making the head-dresses: having tied the twine and brought the straws together to make a cone, he twisted the ends of the straws to make the topknots, which branched out like triple horns. Later, with a good pile of straws made, there was a general adjournment to the pub once more.

Painting the banner pole

Hobby horse frame

Preparations continued in Ciaran Cleary's on Sunday. The frame of the hobby was prepared and more straw suits were made. In the past, the hoops of fish barrels — used in the once substantial cured fish trade — were used for making the hobby, and its body was a good deal larger than the present-day Dingle examples. Its white linen covering was sewn onto the frame by a tailor. In general, the preparations of thirty, forty and fifty years ago were more painstaking and continued for up to three months before the Wren's day. Of course, before the advent of television in the homes of Dingle, and before the relative prosperity of the 1960s, there was little to do to pass the long winter's nights. Some frequented the card schools which still flourish in their season, others just sat at home around the fire, perhaps listening to the radio. And with the onset of winter thoughts turned to the Wren, to the materials to be used for costumes. Satin was the most fancied material and minds dwelt long on consideration of what kind of rig would be made, before cutting and sewing occupied the nights at home. So complete would the rigs be, with the aim that no person should be recognisable by their neighbours, that no item of the person's everyday clothing was visible and even hands were gloved.

Making straws, 26 December

John Benny Moriarty, a teacher in Westmeath and a member of the Green and Gold band, painted cardboard signs for the float: "Rape of the Ranga" was his theme, and when Fergus suggested that "Rape" be changed to "Wreck" there were a few cries of "censorship", but a new piece of cardboard was found and "Wreck" was the word on the day.

In the yard behind, Purdge and John Greaney worked to brush up the float as the daylight died. A broken dinghy lying nearby was pressed into service as a representation of the Ranga.

Indoors, Peter O'Regan carried out repairs on the drums, tied the white ropes onto the side drums, and painted the words "Green and Gold" on the big drum.

There was an air of formality as the final night of preparations was rounded off with a tune. But, of course, the night was not yet over and Paddy Bawn's was only round the corner. While John Murphy made a drum of the table, Peter O'Regan, John Moriarty and Fergus played their fifes till all ears rang.

The fifes are in B flat, which has posed a problem in recent years because they are difficult to come by. In the natural course of events a number have been lost over the years, many of these taken back to England as souvenirs by visiting emigrants; and it has proved very difficult to find replacements. Two which had belonged to a similar band were acquired in about 1972 from the Skibbereen area. Fifes heard in Dublin by Fergus were tracked down to Rann na Feirste in Donegal, but the people there, who had got their own from an Orange band in the Six Counties, were not selling. Peter O'Regan has recently tried his hand at making some but has so far been unable to obtain ebony, from which the original fifes are made, and so has settled for the moment for Iroko, a teak.

It may seem incongruous that the B flat fife should be an important element of the Dingle Wren, for it is primarily associated with the Orange, or British Loyalist bands of Northern Ireland. Dingle, in the extreme south-west, may be said to possess as solidly Catholic, Republican and Gaelic a tradition as any part of Ireland. But one of the consequences of its economic deprivation over recent centuries was a high rate of enlistment in the British armed forces.

The music of the Green and Gold represents a distinct tradition in Dingle, imported, probably in the nineteenth century, by men from Dingle who had served in British army bands. It has no affinity with the background of the general musical tradition of the Dingle area. The instruments — fife and drum — are those of army bands, and the tunes that are characteristic of the Wren were popular in the eighteenth and nineteenth centuries in Ireland and Scotland. It is an essentially urban music of a kind that marching bands all over Ireland would have played.

An incident which illustrates its army associations occurred in 1921. Playing the tune known as "Old Comrades" as he passed the forge in Holy Ground, Michael Graham was surprised to have suddenly thrust into his hand the then princely sum of five shillings. Its donor, it transpired, was an English ex-soldier visiting Dingle who had sadly concluded that the Irish detested everything British until he heard this tune which gladly recalled for him his days in the British Army.

Fifes resting on turf briquettes

given particular impetus in Dingle by the impact of the filming of *Ryan's Daughter* in 1968.

Those who grew up in Dingle in the period up to about 1968 inhaled, by and large, an atmosphere of underdevelopment, of the hard economic reality that their own home town offered only poverty. Knowing that it was impossible to make a living in their own place, they were hardly likely to feel a great sense of commitment and engagement. For those who have grown up since, the significant rise in prosperity, so marked in contrast to the poverty of previous generations, has undoubtedly been reflected in greater social confidence.

New opportunities in employment, education and leisure have had a marked and sometimes contradictory effect. New profitability in farming saw a mushrooming of new houses and car ownership increased rapidly. Not only money but an element of self-consciousness in the eyes of the world were injected by the making of the film. Outsiders settled in the area, established businesses, and the flow of tourists from many different countries increased. Perhaps influenced by the evident appreciation of the area by outsiders, drawing upon elements of a declining traditional culture which yet had enough of a glow of life to catch the attention of the young, some people began to look more positively at their home town.

One change in the Wrens which has occurred in recent years is that in about 1975 the collections started to be made for charities. The custom of using the money for barrels of drink, for paying the musicians, and for ball nights was felt to be outdated. People had enough money to buy their own drink and those who were being asked to give began to question why they should sponsor others' drinking.

By noon on Monday, the day of the Wren, the materials prepared in Ciaran Cleary's had been moved into O'Flaherty's and the first pints of a long day's drinking were already being despatched. Straws lay piled on tables and during the next hour some asked if they might take them to wear, others just took them. Tom Long was using the top of the pool table as a workbench while he prepared the hobby horse. Nearby sat Michael Graham with his two sons, Danny and Ian, both teachers in Limerick. Michael Graham's heyday as a Wrenboy was in the 1920s. An accomplished footballer, he led out a Football Wren for some years, but from 1924 "the youth that would go on it emigrated in a flood". He played the accordion himself, and while the fife was the traditional instrument, dance music on the accordion also proved very popular.

In parts of Kerry and Cork the hobby horse was often known as the Láir Bhán (white mare) and was once associated with All Hallow's Eve and in some instances Bealtaine (May Day) and St. John's Eve. In Dingle it is sometimes called the capall bán or the capallín bán. It has a pedigree which may be traced down the centuries through most of Europe. Close parallels exist in the *Mari Luyd* of Wales and the *laare vane* of the Isle of Man. The *Mari Luyd*, or grey mare, was a horse's skull with snapping jaws on a pole carried by a man covered with a white sheet, and it was part of Christmas folk custom in South Wales. Among the earlier associations of the Láir Bhán may be the notion of sovereignty, particularly in relation to fertility. In the twelfth-century *Topographia Hibernica* of Giraldus Cambrensis there is a remarkable description of an Irish kingship initiation ceremony.

There is in the northern part of Ulster, namely in Kenelcunell [Tyrconnel], a certain people which is accustomed to consecrate its king in a rite altogether outlandish and abominable. When the people of that land had been gathered together in one place, a white mare is brought forward into the midst of the assembly. He who is to be inaugurated, not as chief but as beast, not as king but as an outlaw, embraces the animal before all, professing himself to be a beast also. The mare is then killed immediately, cut up in pieces and boiled in water. A bath is prepared for the man afterwards in the same water. He sits in the bath surrounded by all the people and all, they and he, eat of the meat which is

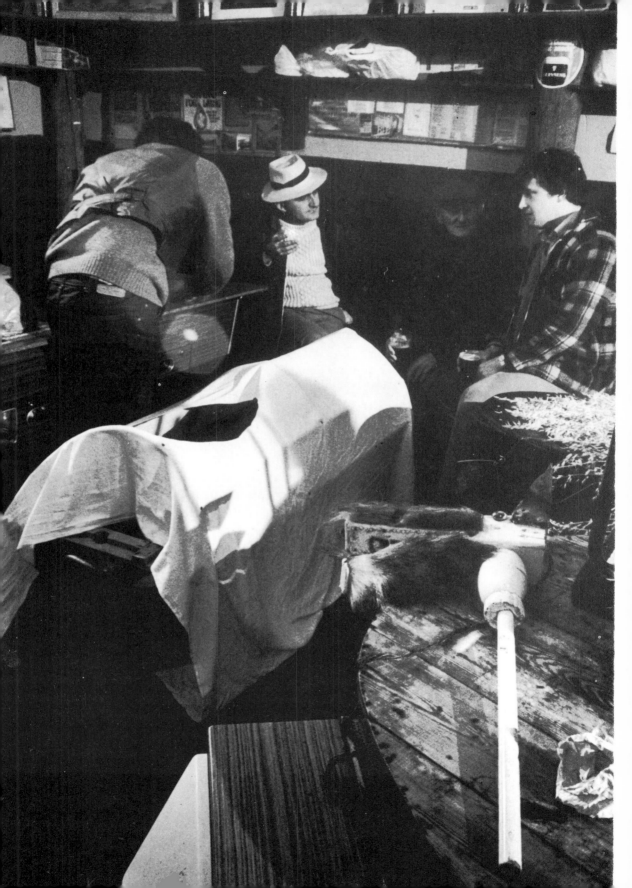

brought to them. He quaffs and drinks of the broth in which he is bathed, not in any cup or using his hand but just dipping his mouth into it round about. When this unrighteous rite has been carried out his kingship and dominion has been conferred.[6]

Marie Louise Sjoestedt, in *Gods and Heroes of the Pagan Celts* (trans. Myles Dillon), suggests that this ritual association of the white mare, fertility and kingship, belongs to the most ancient level of Indo-European religion, and she cites a similar ritual from India described in the Hindu *Aśvamedha*, although in this case it is the king's wife who lies down through a whole night with a dead horse, to the accompaniment of ribald remarks and long laughter.

It is impossible to say with any certainty that there is a direct link between the white mare of the kingship initiation ritual and the Láir Bhán, or hobby horse. However, there is clear evidence that the custom of people dressing as horses as part of festivities in the time around 1 January existed as early as the first century A.D. and persisted with considerable vigour for many centuries in many European countries. Saint Augustine said in a sermon in the early fifth century, "If you ever hear of anyone carrying on that most filthy habit of dressing up like a horse or a stag, punish him most severely." Church leaders had occasion frequently over succeeding centuries to denounce this remnant of pagan religion; but by the sixteenth century, the role of the horse and of animal masks had developed away from its pagan origins. It became then, in the sixteenth and seventeenth centuries, a prominent and less scandalous part of folk custom, a popular element in England in May-time morris dancing and in processions of many kinds in England, Spain, Portugal and other countries.

In O'Flaherty's pub Tom Long checked the hooped ribs of the hobby's frame and pinned the white sheet on it; the head, with its string for pulling the jaws together, lay nearby. Tom Moriarty of Moriarty's the butchers was jumping around wearing a straw skirt and a satin top. Paudie Graham, a worker in the boatyard and Captain

O'Flaherty's

of the Wren, wore a dazzlingly multi-coloured knitted dress. Everywhere there were smiles of anticipation, people putting on motley clothes, carrying and holding things, exchanging greetings. Fergus alternatively pottered and bustled, checking out fifes and drums, taking a fife in one hand and smacking it into the palm of the other. A boy wearing a straw suit over pyjamas played a tin whistle.

By one o'clock the pub was crowded and speculation, suggestion and counter-suggestion were rife as to what would be the starting time. For the next half hour there was much movement between the bar and the street outside. Tom Long brought the hobby out and placed it against the wall opposite at the entrance to the Garda station; people stood talking in the road and on the pavement; musicians warmed up with a few tunes in front of the door.

John Murphy, Martin Flannery, Peter O'Regan,
Fergus O'Flaherty, and John Benny Moriarty

Martin Flannery and John Murphy played the side drums, providing the distinctive marching beat that was to echo through the day
and night. Martin, with his white hair falling over his forehead from
his angled cap, and with his pipe held in the corner of his mouth or
tucked into his breast pocket, is a personification of the Dingle
marching band tradition. An excellent pilot who is accustomed, on
reaching the mouth of Dingle harbour, to ask angling parties, "Is it
east for fish or west for glory?" he is the subject of many anecdotes.

John Murphy, whose first year in Dingle it was, combined so well
with Martin Flannery, the veteran bandsman, that one would have
thought he had been a Green and Gold drummer for years.

John Greaney hitched the float to his car and brought it from the
back yard to the street, and Mary Mazz applied her artistic skills to
painting "Ranga" on the bows of the battered dinghy. Among the
slogans attached to the float was "Pollution No Solution". The float's
theme was the wrecking of the Ranga, a cargo container ship which
came to grief at Dunmore Head at the extreme south-west of the

Dingle peninsula in March 1982. In a remarkable night's work, a rescue team from Dingle and Dunquin succeeded in getting a line from the cliff to the ship and seven of the crew were brought to safety by breeches buoy. An Air/Sea Rescue helicopter from the British RAF station at Haverfordwest in Wales succeeded in fighting its way through the storm and took off the remaining seven members of the crew.

The Ranga had been carrying oil as ballast and the following day the rocks and cliffs were daubed a shiny black to a considerable height. More oil continued to pollute the outstandingly beautiful beach of Coumeenole in the following months as different authorities disclaimed responsibility. Finally, a salvage company removed some oil in October shortly before the ship was broken in two by new storms. The stern section remained poised on rocks at the foot of the cliff.

The float trailer, as in the previous year, was borrowed from Tralee where it is used in the annual "Rose of Tralee" festival. In the past, floats were drawn on a cart by a donkey and were constructed entirely in Dingle, most notably by the late Michael Quirke. In 1933

The wreck of the Ranga

a cow took the place of a float, and on its side was painted "The best beef is free beef", a reference to the provision of free meat to people collecting unemployment benefit. In 1936 Mrs Casey of Casey's Hotel and the John Street Wren mounted the float dressed as Mrs Simpson, who had married the British King Edward VIII; and in 1938, the year Joe Louis won the world heavyweight championship, a local character known as Johnny Eat-a-Bite featured as the "Great White Hope".

Like the floats, costumes and false faces are also often topical. In 1934, when the birth of the Dionne quintuplets had been in the news, a collective effort featured five dolls, five prams and five nurses. An entire Wren went out in the 1950s as the Ku Klux Klan, and the late 1970s saw a flourishing of Jimmy Carter and Ayatollah Khomeini masks, which were still being worn in 1982, along with masks and costumes representing Miss Piggy and other characters from The Muppets.

The topical references of the float and the masks in Dingle have a parallel in Up-Helly Aa, the Shetlands festival:

> The themes refer to subjects of historical, humorous and topical importance, whether international or local, and often provide satirical comments. [7]

> History and current affairs leave their mark upon the festival and are reflected in it. In 1909 a squad appeared as Suffragettes and 30 years later another group dressed as Hitler's Storm Troopers. [8]

This topicality is also found in the New Year's Eve Fire Festival at Allendale in Northumberland in England:

> Today the appearance of the guysers remains an important feature of New Year's Eve, and there is one group whose members customarily work together to create something of topical interest. In 1970 seven appeared dressed as candles, a reminder of the severe cuts in power experienced that winter. [9]

Bridge Street

The number of people — about 100 — who set out on the first round of the town from Bridge Street was the largest anyone could remember on the Green and Gold. Everyone wore costumes of one kind or another — some elaborate, some simple — and false faces ranged from masks of animals and of public figures to pillowcases with holes for eyes and mouths. Three girls wore green and gold capes. A figure all in white held up an enormous wooden spoon. Fergus O'Flaherty's black hair was roughly covered by a wig of long yellow hair and he wore a yellow cape. Tom Lynch was dressed in a bright green and yellow dress and a yellow paper hat. Peter O'Regan was in his "Fidel Castro" outfit. Purdge, carrying one of the banner poles, had a green and gold scarf tied around his head, a stocking mask and white trousers with yellow ties at the knees. There was Miss Piggy and Kermit the Frog, Jimmy Carter and the Ayatollah Khomeini, gorillas, fanciful mixtures of military uniform with dresses of curtain material. Strong winter sunlight emphasised the bright colours and contributed to the cheerfulness of the parade as it moved off, preceded by the hobby, and turned into the Mall.

The first tune played by the band of the Green and Gold is always "The Old March", and as it proceeds around the town the changes are rung on marches such as "The Days That Are Gone", "Wrap The Green Flag", "O'Neill's" and "The Star of the County Down".

On the left of the Mall the Dingle river flows down to Hudson's Bridge; in reality it is a mere stream, only occasionally and briefly being transformed into something more like a river when heavy rains from hills and fields to the north of the town cascade in a brown torrent. On the right the houses are set back; it is an open street, and the music of the fifes and drums which had seemed strong and expressive outside O'Flaherty's sounded thin in the Mall as it scattered without resonance. The parade had yet to warm up as it passed the monument to those from Dingle who died in the War of Independence, moved passed the former Protestant school and the squat, brown sandstone courthouse, behind which stands the monastery and school of the Christian Brothers.

At the end of the Mall, where John Street and Main Street meet at the bridge, a colourful crowd had gathered, most of them members of Wrens from the Castlegregory area in the north of the peninsula. The parade turned into Main Street and as it marched up the hill past Dykegate Lane the music of the band and shouts of the marchers began to bounce back and forth between the solid lines of substantial houses on either side of the street. Nevertheless, it was a subdued parade, perhaps awed by its own numbers, perhaps a little self-conscious at the presence of the video camera and my own constant photographing, and it maintained its two organised lines as it climbed past Benner's Hotel and the two banks. The large banner was stalwartly held, the hobby turned and pranced, the Captain wielded his sword; the musicians, the float, the marchers in bright costumes and false faces, and the rustling strawboys — all seemed to anticipate festivity; but one sensed restraint; festivity had yet to enter in.

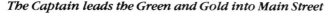

The Captain leads the Green and Gold into Main Street

At the Temperance Hall, where pool tables provide a social centre for many of Dingle's young people, the march swung left past the old presbytery, on the site of which once stood the highest building in the town where rooms are said to have been prepared to accommodate the ousted Queen Marie Antoinette of France. Moving on down Green Street, where small plaques on the walls of houses are believed to be the relics of a once significant Spanish trading presence, the parade passed the nineteenth century Catholic church and the library. At the foot of Green Street it turned right into Strand Street, and now, in this narrow street in the heart of the town, the music, movement and colour became forceful and loud, even strident.

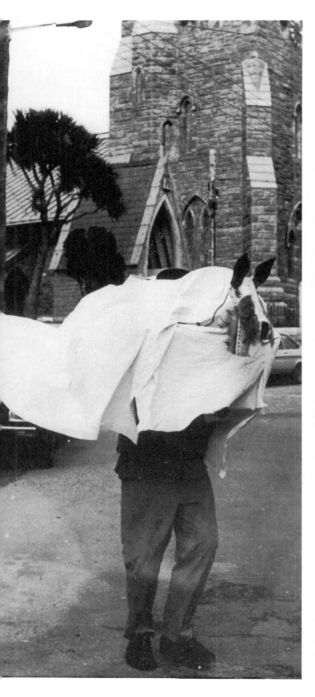

Moving towards the head of the pier and the boatyard, the Green and Gold approached what used to be the territory of the Quay Wren, at one time the biggest and arguably the best of the Dingle Wrens. It was organised by the fishermen of the Quay from Pat Devane's shed which stood opposite Michael Long's public house; this shed, used as a store for nets, was taken over in the later stages of the Civil War by Free State troops. However, not even the War of Independence and the Black and Tans interfered with the holding of the Wren, and the first thirty years of the century were always lively on St Stephen's Day. In the years before 1920, early in the morning, well before sunrise, the adherents of the Quay Wren gathered at Pat Devane's shed and set off for Lord Ventry's house in Burnham, at the western shore of the harbour. "Brian Boru's March" was always played as they made their way and on the high notes many would throw their caps in the air. The first Wren to arrive at the house received the most money (memories of how much vary considerably), and it is said that Lord Ventry was particularly pleased if the Quay were first. The fishermen who made up the Wren were his tenants for the most part, and it was he who sponsored regattas. In popular memory, the trip to Burnham in the early hours of the morning is recalled as one of the most important events and aspects of the day. Money was very scarce; everyone who speaks of the Wrens of that time mentions that "You must remember, there was no money in them days". The Wren was about collecting money, and Lord Ventry's contribution could be as much as ten per cent of the amount collected in the whole day. Nevertheless, Michael Graham suggests that the trip to Burnham was abandoned several years before Lord Ventry's departure in 1920; it is not clear whether people simply no longer had the taste for the long walk in the morning or it seemed less appropriate with the rise of Republicanism.

The music of the Quay Wren was provided by two fifes and two drums; when short of fifes, which were scarce, piano accordions were pressed into service, but these, according to John Joe Sheehy, an active member of the Quay Wren in his youth, were "a dead loss compared to the fifes". Sometimes tin whistles were substituted for fifes, but this was "the easy way out — any fool can play the tin whistle". Straw suits were a constant feature, and they were made in one night, but the straw had to be stolen. Everyone wore a rig of one kind or another — without a proper rig they would not be allowed to join the Wren — and the element of disguise was vital. "You wouldn't know who you'd be next to," says John Joe Sheehy, "by my solemn oath, you would not."

No Quay Wren would be complete without a hobby horse and a donkey and car. The Captain was inside the car with the collecting box, and the car was decorated with holly and ivy, flags and bunting. Until about thirty years ago many of those on the Wren carried on the end of a stick a pig's, cow's or sheep's bladder which they used to hit people over the head.

As a fishermen's Wren, it was natural that the oars of canoes (the canvas-covered naomhóg, elsewhere in Ireland called a curragh) should be used for banner poles; but in earlier years oars were also used in fights between rival groups. This aspect of the Wren does not seem to have survived beyond the end of the last century, and no one alive today recalls it, but second-hand accounts suggest that the fighting was to a certain extent formalised, and while it was briefly violent, it was engaged in without any serious malice.

It was about thirty years ago that the Quay Wren declined. There was a falling out amongst the people who organised it, and it had been weakened by an offshoot, the Garraí Wren, which was based in the group of houses called the Garraí, west of the pier, and which specialised in elaborate costumes. On a couple of occasions in the last twenty years the Quay and Garraí Wrens were briefly revived, but many who had supported them had emigrated, and a few had transferred their allegiance to the Green and Gold. About fifty or sixty years ago the Quay Wren had commanded the support of about sixty-five participants and collected about £10 in the day. The Green and Gold in the same period had slightly fewer followers but always collected about £2 more.

John Joe Sheehy, who is in his seventies, never saw anyone kill a wren, nor saw a wren carried around on St Stephen's Day, but in his youth he heard from older people that the hunting of the wren had been a feature in the last century, and that the Wren with a bird up on a stick would get more money from Lord Ventry than one without it. In *The Year in Ireland* Kevin Danaher quotes a January

1894 note in *The Graphic* entitled "With the Wren Boys in Dingle":

The Wren Boys, having killed a wren tie it to a holly bush on a pole. Two of them decorate their heads and shoulders with straw and wear masks with single eyeholes. These also carry large bladders tied to sticks with which to clear the way. Two others also masked, dress in petticoats and are supposed to represent dancers; six more carry flags, while one plays a fife and another a drum.

Two aspects of the Wren in John Joe's prime as a Wrenboy which no longer pertain took place before and after St Stephen's Day. For the two Sundays prior to the day, the musicians of the Wrens would parade around the town at about 7.30 in the evening. Also, some days after St Stephen's Day, there would be a "ball night". The Quay Wren held theirs in the cinema in Dykegate Lane, which was also a dancehall. Currant loaf and tea and what was called a "scrap dance" were features of these ball nights, but they fell foul of priestly opposition. Fifty years ago Father Sullivan condemned the holding of ball nights by the Quay and John Street Wrens and that year no one came. These were the "Hungry 'Thirties" when a population struggling against conditions of extreme poverty and bled dry by the emigration of its most active members submitted to the authority of a militantly puritanical church. Even patrons at holy wells were discouraged and Father Lynch broke up the platform dancing. The church held sway and ball nights all over the peninsula became confined to houses sufficiently isolated from the priests' ken. But they were not suppressed entirely and there are those who remember Father Sullivan leaning despondently as he gripped the pulpit and intoned sadly: "It has come to my notice that there was a ball night in a place called Ballinaboula, and that my intentions were thwarted."

Many Wrens in recent years have gone no further than the Star Inn at the head of the pier, but in 1982 the Green and Gold carried on past the Star Inn, past Ó Catháin's fish plant to the end of the cottages at An Choill. For John Joe Sheehy, who lives in one of the cottages, this was a sign of a good Wren, but he was also impressed by the numbers, by the music of the fifes and drums, and by the quality of the rigs. Many older people will say, understandably, that the Wrens have declined since their young days, but John Joe suggested that the Green and Gold of 1982 was the best in fifty or sixty years.

At the cottages the band played "Old Comrades", a version of "I Lost My Love", which was collected in County Clare by George Petrie, the antiquary, painter and musician, whose *The Ancient Music of Ireland* was published in 1855.

And as they returned along the Quay, the tune was

Take her away down to the Quay,
We don't want her at all today.

This tune is known elsewhere as "I Won't Marry Her", with the words:

I won't marry her, I won't marry her,
She's too bold, I'm too old
And I won't marry her at all, at all:
I won't marry her at all, at all.

The parade turned at the cottages and marched back the way it had come, and some made their first stop for drink at the Star Inn at the head of the pier, others at Murphy's; but the main body of marchers entered Paddy Bawn's in Strand Street. Now, as the pub was packed out with shouting, jostling and laughing revellers, the day was really beginning, the pints of Guinness offering the taste of many more to come. Some people were laughing, joking, pulling at each other's costumes; others set up a shout like the yelping of a

In Green Street

pack of hounds. Those sitting down inside the pub in their ordinary clothes were jeered at from behind false faces; costumed figures stood with hands raised in threatening gestures as they taunted and teased people who could not recognise them. Fergus, his lank blond wig askew on his head, marshalled members of the band who struck up a tune which competed with shouts of greeting and mockery and the laughter which burst in waves from all sides. Children looked goggle-eyed at the costumed revellers: some laughed with delight into masked faces while others clung fearfully to parents; one unfortunate child erupted into wails of anguish as he backed away from the monstrous invasion.

The first round of the town had now been completed, and the float was brought back to the yard. Most of the crowd had been winkled out of the pub and the Green and Gold set off up Green Street. After passing the church, they struck up the following tune, about which Fergus O'Flaherty said, "You could call it 'Stony Hill' if you wanted a name for it, but the way we call it, we just say: 'We'll play this one, then . . .', you know. There's a version of it on a De Danaan record: Charlie Piggott picked it up from the Flannerys, who'd be his uncles, I suppose." An amalgam of tunes, it is basically a version of the eighteenth century "Rose Tree", starting with a piece from "Leather Away the Wattle-o!"

At the top of Green Street it turned left into Upper Main Street. Here it stopped at Lynch's, home base of the Goat Street Wren, and it was as well that quite a number had fallen by the wayside for Lynch's is hardly the largest of Dingle's fifty-two pubs. Here the cry from Fergus was that there would be one swift drink only before continuing up the hill to the hospital.

It was an opportunity to cool down after the climb from Strand Street and relax in the bright winter sunlight. The heavy material of many costumes and the false faces of plastic and rubber had caused many to work up a healthy sweat. False faces were raised, straw headgear removed and drums placed on the pavement as the wrenboys took their ease in the street. But whoever was wearing the full gorilla suit preserved his identity intact.

The Holey Stone

Most of the Green and Gold soon left Lynch's and, striking uphill, the band played "Humpty Dumpty", their name for a setting of "The Kinnegad Slashers", which is featured in many eighteenth century collections of Irish music. Children, their arms linked in groups of three or four, pranced and danced in the street as they climbed the hill, up past the "Holey Stone" — a *bullaun* or large boulder with hollows in which, it is thought, corn was ground in the early Christian period — to Goat Street and on to the hospital.

The band of the Green and Gold at the top of Goat Street

In the hospital there was a welcome from the nurses as the human
tide of marchers, headed now by the musicians, flowed through the
corridors into the wards. Most of the patients were elderly, and
memories were stirred of their own youthful capers on St Stephen's
Day.

A drab institutional building, Dingle hospital, in common with hospitals in other small towns, lacks funds for modernisation, and for many medical services patients are transferred to Tralee or Cork. Despite the best efforts of the staff, there is a gloomy air about the place, and there was something incongruous, even bizarre, about the brief presence of the Wrenboys within its confines. The jostling crowd in their wild and colourful rigs contrasted with two-tone grey walls as they bobbed in and out of the wards, sat on beds, greeted patients and played their music.

In one of the first-floor wards twelve-year-old Niamh O'Donnell in her green and yellow cape danced where dazzling shafts of light struck the floor. Two years before, Niamh had also danced in the hospital, and there had been a poignancy about the occasion. In the hospital then was Padraig Ó Siochrú who, many years before, had taught her mother to dance to "The Blackbird". At the end of his life, young Niamh, as she danced to the same tune, must have brought a special joy to the old man.

Downstairs, Fergus talked to Mrs O'Flaherty of Ventry, tragically to die a few months later; and her radiant smile seemed a triumphant justification of the visit.

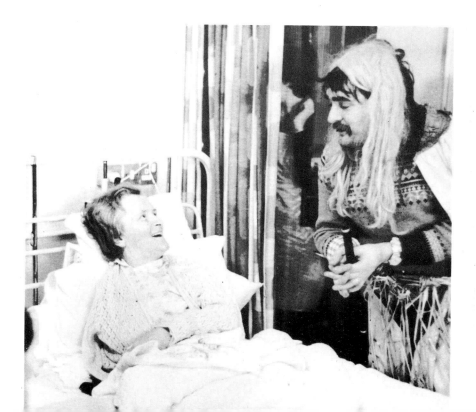

The John Street Wren in Green Street

As the Green and Gold left the hospital, the John Street Wren was arriving with twenty or thirty members, and prominent amongst them was Weeshy Murphy, doggedly carrying the battered frame of a hobby horse which had lost its covering. The Sráid Eoin, or John Street, Wren differs considerably from the Green and Gold and is regarded by many as having had the best tradition of all Wrens in this century. In recent years it has been less organised than the Green and Gold, fewer people follow it and the rigs are generally less elaborate.

John Street stands at what was until the late 1830s the main entrance from the east to the town. Those who speak of the tradition of the Sráid Eoin Wren recall first and foremost the particular individuals who gave it its unique character. Tommy the Gabha (Blacksmith) and Muirris the Gabha — two O'Sullivan brothers — Mikey Casey, the Farrells, Paddy Hanafin, Frank Carroll and the Lynches are names synonymous with this Wren in the past. John Ferriter, known to all as "the Kerryman", was its legendary organiser, its heart and soul, for many years, and the shed behind Rohan's pub was where the preparations were made. The bagpipes were a particular feature, but this part of the tradition died in about 1950 when Mikey Casey gave up playing them. Both the Kerryman and Frank Carroll worked on the roads, the Kerryman as a "surface man" and Frank Carroll as a ganger laying pavements. Frank was cashier for several years and always took from the collection one pound to give to the priest to say mass for members of the Wren who had died.

Rohan's, John Street

After the musicians and banner carriers had been paid, the rest of the money in his time went towards the purchase of a firkin of porter for the lads. He was also noted for the rigs he made: "My father was a tailor and I was handy with a needle myself. Without exaggeration I went to a lot of trouble making rigs."

Prominent amongst the musicians of the present day John Street Wren are Anton, Peter and Larry Flannery, maintaining a family tradition. Anton recalls his father, Charlie, talking about an Englishman, Joe Gorman, an ex-soldier who had taught "them all" to play. He had, it was said, played before the British King and Queen, and it was he who had trained Tim and Paddy Healy, Charlie Flannery, the Sweeneys and others who formed the backbone of Dingle's marching bands. Although members of rival Wrens are rarely profuse in praise for each other, Fergus O'Flaherty readily acknowledges his debt to John Street which kept the tradition alive when other Wrens had declined. The person most universally credited with maintaining it was the Kerryman, who could be seen on the day in his suit of straws with a Guinness sign on his back, and who, as many people recall, "lived for the Wren". And credit too, is given to Maurice Rohan, who organised the Wren in the '60s and '70s. Now living in County Clare, Maurice would never dream of missing the Wren, and he recalls how in John Street it was such a tradition that a week would not pass through the year in which some reference would not be made to it. "Everything else was compared to it. You might see a picture in a newspaper or a film on television, and someone would say that face or whatever it was would go well in the Wren."

Leaning on the bar across the outside of the window of O'Connor's shop at the foot of John Street, he can point to each house in view and recite how each of them supported the Wren through the years. Involved now in exploring, studying and promoting traditional culture in County Clare, it is clear that his heart will always lie with the tradition of his own street in Dingle.

Until recent years the straws of the Sráid Eoin were the best of all Wrens. The pick of the oats was provided by a number of farms which were regular supporters. "They were a great crowd in John Street," says Paudie Curran, who was one of the mainstays of the Green and Gold in his youth, "for keeping the tradition, and they were the only ones in town that could make the straws." The making of the straw suits constituted a large part of the attraction and enjoyment of the Wren. Barrels of porter were consumed while the straws were made in Rohan's, and an advantage of being involved was that drink would be available, too, on Christmas Day, a "black" day when pubs were closed. As Paudie Curran puts it, "It was a porter Wren."

The first call on money collected by the Wren would be to meet the bill for porter, presented by the publican even before the parade moved off on St Stephen's Day. And when it came to collecting money, the Sráid Eoin came off well because it had the best characters. But in the 1930s and '40s collecting was done only from house to house, for anyone in a pub lucky enough to have the price of a drink would have no pennies left over.

A man with a memory of the John Street Wren of the 1920s is John Farrell of the Spa Well pub in Spa Road. The break between the 1920s and the 1930s was a traumatic one, for almost everyone involved in organising the Wren in the 1920s was forced by the poverty of the times to emigrate, as did John Farrell himself in 1927, returning to Dingle in 1974. Laughingly contemptuous of the "bunch of yobs" that go out on the modern Wrens, he takes no interest in them. But he recalls with evident enthusiasm and relish the days when there were sixteen pipers on the John Street Wren. He remembers too, going out as an old woman dressed in his grandmother's check apron, with a red petticoat and elastic shoes, a grey wig, shawl and cape, and a mask of an old woman's face. "I was the tallest woman ever on the Wren." An active Republican, in 1923 he was Captain of a special Wren, the Dreoilín Beag Sinn Féin, which was made up of members of the Fianna, the Republican boys' organisation.

The long tradition of the John Street Wren is best and most briefly summed up in the catch-cry of the late Paddy Hanafin: "Up Sráid Eoin! We never died a winter yet and the devil himself wouldn't kill us in the summer."

As the Green and Gold passed down Main Street again from the hospital, the debris of straws carpeting the street outside Lynch's was attracting small birds, clusters of which could be seen there for the rest of the day enjoying the unexpected feast.

Approaching John Street, the band played a tune later christened "Slaudeen's Delight" when it was included on a record – "Forever by Dingle Shore" by Slaudeen – which featured several of the Green and Gold Wren musicians. The first part of this tune is generally known as "Sweet Biddy Daly".

After stopping for a while at the foot of John Street, they moved off along The Mall, and here the tune was a version of the eighteenth century Scottish "Lass of Gowrie".

By this time the Aughacasla and Tullig Wrens, from the north of the peninsula, had gathered their forces and were in command of Strand Street. The difference between these two Wrens and those of the town was evident. The bands played accordions and bodhrans; there were no straw suits; and the main elements of costume were pyjamas and decorated hats. The hobby horses were considerably larger than those of the Green and Gold, Sráid na Gabhar (Goat Street) and Sráid Eoin Wrens, with long necks which were, like the bodies, covered with white sheeting.

About twenty years ago there occurred a substantial decline in the Wren's day custom on the north of the peninsula, and during the 1960s and 1970s only the Tullig Wren continued to organise. However, in 1980, the local community council sponsored a revival of the custom and adopted the North Kerry fashion of having polka set competitions between different Wren groups. This proved an effective spur, and in 1982 there were four Wrens, followed by about forty people each. There is a feeling that the revival has brought with it an inappropriate competitiveness, and aggravation that occurred in Castlegregory on St Stephen's Day in 1982 is deplored by many. But while revival has caused some change the main elements of the custom, and the differences with Dingle, are still evident.

In the Castlegregory area the focus of the Wren is primarily on the "ball nights" which occur a few days later. The day itself is devoted to collecting money around the houses, and this money is used to finance the ball night. Straw suits are regarded as having been traditional, but they were not made for many years until the Tullig Wren was inspired by the competition to revive the art in 1980 and 1981. The hobby horses were made recently but followed the style of previous hobbies which had become worn out. There is no local memory of wrens being hunted or bladders on sticks. In many parts of the country the Wren's day featured a series and a variety of rhymes; this aspect of the custom has all but died out in Corca Dhuibhne, but in the Castlegregory area the children recite as they call to houses:

The Wren, the Wren, the king of all birds
On Stephen's Day was caught in the furze,
So up with the kettles and down with the pans
And give us a penny to bury the wren.

A longer rhyme, given in Mr and Mrs Hall's *Ireland* (1841) goes as follows:

The wran, the wran, the king of all birds,
St Stephen's day was cot in the furze

Although he is little his family's grate,
Put yer hand in yer pocket and give us a trate.
  Sing holly, sing ivy — sing ivy, sing holly,
    A drop just to drink it would drown melancholy
And if you dhraw it ov the best,
    I hope in heaven yer sowl will rest,
    But if you dhraw it ov the small
It won't agree wid de wran boys at all.

In the past there were more Wrens, each of which had fewer
followers than the present count of about forty; and the all-important
ball nights — held these days in hotels and pubs — were celebrated
in particular houses in almost every townland between Brandon
and Camp. A song which is sung by John Joe Gleeson of Meenascorthy and which he says he picked up from Mikey Mansell of
nearby Duagh in the late 1920s or early 1930s is called "The Ball
Without the Tea".

Come all ye lads and lasses and come listen to the song,
Oh, I'm both sad and mournful, sure, I can't detain you long:
It is all about a Wren ball, we're sorry for to say,
'Tis carried out by the neighbourhood, called the Ball Without
    the Tea.

The people came from many a place, from Derrymore and Camp,
And little Mary Griffin, now, that travelled through the swamp;
But when they got up to the door one-and-six they had to pay
For to get into the cabin of the Ball Without the Tea.

Now, Deelis boys they organised and said they would take the
    trip:
Mikey Knightey, Tim the Captain, and the orders were slow-whip,
But when they landed in the yard and heard that they should pay
They busted in the rafters of the Ball Without the Tea.

Now, Andy Long he is the man with a nose so very flat,
You'd swear he was a bog-deal stick you'd stretch across a gap:
He was walking up and down the floor, he was telling them what
    to do,

But 'twas well the people knew our boys, my old hungry-looking
    crew.

We've travelled many a county and we've met with many men,
But such an ugly creature, now, Tim Cota or Yellow Tim:
His little head was shaking, we heard the people say,
They saw nothing but starvation in the Ball Without the Tea.

There was a ball at Meenascorthy by a tailor and a cow,
Myself and Tommy came by bikes, we landed in there now,
But when we entered in the door we heard John Dilker say:
"Take up the boiling kettle and put down the fecking tea!"

He then went up the stairs, he brought the teapot down:
Such a teapot, in my life, was the big one he brought down.
The girls was first to have the tea, they drank it in the round,
And when the tea was over the shillings made a pound.

The boys was next to have the tea, they drank it in the round,
But when he shook the dice, it made a big, big pound.
We had Jim and Jack to sing a song, Jim Hilliard to play the tune,
The boys and girls they danced their 'nough and the day it
    dawned too soon.

The tailor said, "Cut up the bread, give 'em all enough to eat,
But next Sunday night I will be tight below near Beolan's beat."
The tailor then sat down to eat, for I made no mistake,
Out of the bottom of a press he pulled a nice fruit cake.

As long as I'm a rover I'll think of this ball night;
I was invited to another in Glan Lough above the height.
When I landed in the yard I thought 'twas the devil's den,
I was neither told to stop outside or neither ushered in.

I said I'd see the party but 'twas then I got a fright,
For a man without a nose stood up and said I wasn't wanted here
    tonight.
I then picked up my coat and jumped on my machine,
With a weakness in my heart for tea I struck for old Canneen.

'Twas here I finished up until I see the day,
May God help the boys that stuck it out in the Ball Without the
    Tea! [10]

The ball nights that are held these days are very different affairs, some of them providing their own music, others bringing bands in from outside, but all in the Castlegregory area taking place in hotels and pubs.

Having had their Wrens in 1982 on the Sunday of St Stephen's Day, Aughacasla and Tullig made a second day of it in Dingle on the Monday. There was admiration from some in Dingle for the hobbies, and there was no doubt that the people from over the hill added life and colour with the accordion and bodhran music and their dancing in the streets.

In Main Street as the light began to fade the unaccustomed music of the banjo combined with accordions, and the dancers turned and turned again outside Benner's Hotel.

In Paddy Bawn's within a milling crowd musicians of the Green and Gold put away their fifes and resorted to the tin whistle while people with costumes in various stages of disarray danced to the music in the confined space and more than one drink went flying. In the street outside some danced to the music of other bands, others stood and watched, talked and drank. A short way down the street from Bawn's a group of lads took a break for a smoke, sitting and standing beside a discarded, headless hobby horse. Wrenboys with collecting boxes elbowed their ways through the tightly packed crowds in Garvey's, crossed the street to Bawn's, remaining only briefly in 'the presence of the Green and Gold contingent and moving on again to Murphy's. The collectors have always been vital to the Wrens, especially in the days when the money went towards the ball night and paying for the drink consumed in making the straws, and their importance was carried over into the term "holly holder", which was once used in general Dingle parlance to describe anyone who held the purse strings in a family. The collecting box in the past was always surrounded by holly and placed in the cart pulled by the donkey.

The Goat Street Wren appeared in Strand Street: having started out with no hobby horse (they had lost its head) and a small contingent, it gathered more of its followers as it paraded with its band of flutes and drums, with Martin, Colm and Enda Kennedy, Patneen Flannery, Brian Scanlon and Michael Dowd. The B flat fife was once the traditional instrument of Goat Street as well as the Green and Gold, but was abandoned in favour of the flute, which is less difficult to play.

In the 1950s this Wren declined: emigration had robbed the street of most of its young men. The houses which once lined the lower side of the street are long demolished, though their front walls, with filled-in-windows and doors, still stand. There was a brief recovery in the Wren, then it did not go out at all between 1963 and 1973, reviving again and being held every year since 1974.

"Sergeant" Houlihan of Chapel Lane, now 73, recalls that in his youth many of the men in the street were ex-soldiers and that they had established, with men like the Healys, a good drumming tradition which they passed on to their sons. "And then the music was in families like the Flannerys, who were fishermen, of course, and the Scanlons, and these families are the same yet." There was little money in Goat Street, yet masks were acquired from Gamages in London and "Sergeant" Houlihan remembers paying one-and-threepence for one. There were sheeps' bladders on sticks and "a few fellas might have them pinned on their front, like women!"

A nonsense rhyme of the Goat Street Wren concerns Sean Gould, whose butcher's shop once stood below Lynch's pub.

All the boys they ran down Goat Street
All the girls they made a plan
All the boys they ran down Goat Street
To kill Sean Gould and the boody man.

Another rhyme goes:

Goat Street gave us Padraig Scanlon
With his belly fat and round
John Street gave us Pad Houlihan
With his one leg on the ground
To lead the boys from Kerry

And to lead the boys from Clare
Wicklow, Dublin, Donegal
And the boys from old Kildare.

Comparing the Green and Gold with the Goat Street Wren, he says, "The Green and Gold were clerks and so on, they were a bit above us, like; naturally, they'd have better rigs because they could afford them."

Many people insist that the oats were longer in their youth and that they made better suits. Certainly, the way in which they were made was somewhat different, and created a thicker garment. The Goat Street Wren made theirs in a shed in Chapel Lane on Christmas Day, and many a gallon of porter was carried up to the shed to aid the work. The hobby horse in the past was a bigger animal than the present-day species in Dingle: "It would be put together like a canoe, and there was always some carpenter had the knack of making its head." With several times its present population in the 1930s, Goat Street was one year able to support two Wrens — one with the traditional elements of straws, hobby and banner, the other a "modern" version called the Aeroplane Wren, for which Michael Quirke, a notable contributor of floats and other Wren decorations, constructed a large model aeroplane.

To the west of Goat Street, Milltown used to support a Wren, but its population has declined dramatically, and the last year it went out was 1953, the year when Christie was hanged. Then, a notable character, a simple man named Johnny the King, who is well remembered in the town, was carried on the cart as Christie. Between ten and twenty went out on the Wren in its final years, wearing all kinds of rigs, but without straws or a hobby.

"Sergeant" Houlihan regrets the decline of the children's Wren in Dingle, which used to go collecting door to door in the morning: "It is watching television they are now, and they have enough of money." But he is pleased to see the adult Wrens kept up: "They're going as good as ever now. People thought they were dead and gone, but they came back very well. The young people have joined up for the bit of a crack."

As the light over the town began to fade from about four o'clock, the evening settled into a pattern of visits to pubs in various parts of

Taking a rest

A lull in Paddy Bawn's

the town, some music inside the pubs and plenty of high-spirited chat, a move out into the streets again after a decent interval for drinking, some music outside and dancing in the streets, further parading, then into another pub.

The Lispole Wren, from east of the town, arrived in Dingle in two groups, with musicians and others mounted on a lorry, the amplified sound of accordions and drums blaring out from loudspeakers. There was no hobby or straw suits and sheets were the most favoured materials for costumes, but they were a very lively crowd as they danced in the streets and marched behind, in front of and around the lorry. Hearing the amplification, one of the Green and Gold musicians remarked, "Next year we'll have a bloody disco Wren!"

Lispole musicians on the lorry

Early in this century there were four Wrens in Lispole parish. Patrick Begley, 76, whose house stands above the bridge at Ballinasare, was an active participant in one of these, the Minard Wren, until the mid-'30s. In his mother's youth the Wrenboys had worn straw suits, carried hobby horses and hunted wrens; but while he can recall being frightened by the hobbies as a child, all these elements had gone from the Lispole Wrens by 1920. The Wrens of Patrick's heyday went from house to house, singing songs, saying rhymes and dancing jigs or hornpipes inside the houses. Each Wren had a Captain and a cashier, and there used to be a bull's horn which was blown at a particular angle to produce a sound which carried down the bohareens and across the hills and fields of the parish.

While many of the traditional elements have gone from the Wren of the present day, the custom has been observed every year without a break in Lispole for at least the last hundred years. "From time to time it might have died down, but it never died out. There'd always be young people going out."

"It was all about collecting money for the ball night," says Patrick Begley. Ball nights were held in many houses in the neighbourhood, and Patrick remembers that the price of a sixteen-gallon barrel of porter in his time was four pounds and five shillings. "We used organise to get the girls. It was very hard in those days to spend any time at all in the company of girls, and we'd organise the ball nights to get the girls. That was the name of the game." But it was a game that invoked the opposition of the Church. The Redemptorist missioners who came to the parish from Limerick denounced all forms of mixed entertainment; the celebrations at the patron of St John the Baptist's Well were suppressed, and in 1927 a priest came out from Dingle in the middle of the night to a ball night in Doonties and broke it up with the aid of his riding crop.

If the Kerryman may be credited with doing much to keep alive the Dingle tradition, credit for maintaining the marching band tradition must go to Dinny Joe Griffin of Lispole. From his trailer workshop he organised in the 1950s and 1960s an accordion marching band, a céilí band and a modern band. There were two Lispole Wrens then and Dinny Joe's marching band, numbering twelve to fourteen, came out on the Dreoilín an Aghasaigh, which was the eastern of the two.

Starting usually at about 9.30 from Lisdargan, they proceeded along the bottom of the hill, then went down to Ballinasare, Minard, Doonties, Ardamore, Coumlanders, Lispole, finishing at Tober in Kinard. Preparations began early, and on evenings in November and December they would parade along the main road from Lispole to Garrynadur. Arriving there, the people living near the road would gather at each crossroads to hear and dance to jigs and reels.

The hobby, or white horse as they called it in Lispole, had lapsed from the Wren but was brought back and Dinny Joe's father showed them how to make it.

In 1957 the Lispole Wren came into Dingle on St Stephen's Day for the first time. "We were shaky coming into Dingle. We were country boys and at that time there was a big division between the town and the country. But we were carried away with the reception we got; it was great. I remember seeing old men jumping off the footpath and joining us marching. We'd march maybe fifty yards and we'd stop then and play céilí music, and there'd be two or three cashiers collecting, and then we'd be off again. The previous year in Lispole they had collected £9; in Dingle in 1957 the takings were £31, and we had the greatest ball night ever in Paddy Griffin's in Ballinisteenig, with people coming from Dingle as well as our own parish. We hadn't known what to expect, we had never seen Dingle Wrens; but all we saw were a couple of fifes and a drum. Some of the Dingle crowd had amplification and they were playing records." Ironically, it is now the Lispole Wren which features amplification, much to the disapproval of many in Dingle.

During the course of the afternoon the Green and Gold had lost the head from its hobby, but Rose Brosnan took over from Tom Long and the headless horse continued its perambulations late into the night. The band played indoors and out on the streets, sometimes exchanging fifes for tin whistles when players found their teeth loosening in their gums with the effort of playing. The musicians were pleased with themselves, for they had enough good and competent players to allow some to take a rest from time to time, though one took an unorthodox kind of a rest when he fell into the sea at the pier; and as they made their periodic sallies into the streets they were able to keep up a remarkably consistent performance.

Musicians of the Green and Gold

On the trailer of An Gaeltacht

The Gaeltacht Wren, from the west, entered the town from Milltown and down Goat Street, with a banner, a tractor and a trailer on which sat musicians and others. For those in the Gaeltacht, in Dunquin, Ballyferriter, Ballydavid and Feohanagh, the main activity of the Wren had been the day before, when children and young people had walked the roads and bohareens calling to houses for

In Ballyferriter

money. A fine insight into the children's Wrens is given in *Jimín Mháire Thaidhg* by Padraig Ó Siochrú, who wrote under the name of 'An Seabhac', and, although fictional, it reflects the custom as it was at the end of the last century.

I got up before everybody else in the morning. I put the elastic shoes under my oxter. Then I went to Cáit's room and searched again for a rig for Tadgh. The Devil tempted me in the end and I took Cáit's dress and other things and out I went through the window and into the stable.

I put on my Wren uniform — the elastic boots and the tail coat and the top hat with Cáit's ribbons flowing from it. I put on my false face then and my belt and sword and I can tell you that I had the appearance of a Wren Captain then if anybody ever had. Off I went then looking for the others. They were coming one by one and none of them recognised me until I took off my false face. We spent a good while organising ourselves until we·were ready. When Tadhg Larry Beag came I tried to put Cáit's clothes on him but there was a knot in the story. Cáit's clothes would not fit him unless he took off his own. This did not please him at all. All that we left on him was his shirt but when the dress was on him and the paper cape on his head he was a girl right enough. The shoes went against him, however. They were his father's pair and were

too big for him. The way it was they were dragging behind him with every flip-flop.

We had four musicians. I had a mouth organ belonging to Cáit which she got from our Aunty. Tomáisín Beag had it to play for the day. Micilín had a tin trumpet which he gave to Smule. Somebody had a great big tin dish and he was at it with a stick. Another had a tin bucket hanging around his neck, and when the four of them were at it all together blowing and drumming and making noise they made fine music.

I gave a holly bush to Peats Micilín Dean and Micilín Eoin had a bladder on a stick which we got from Tadhg Óg when they killed the pig before Christmas: he was hitting everybody with it. Some had sacks on them and others had men's shirts and the odd one had an old skirt of their mother's.

Beit Mór's house was the first place we tried. I had my sword drawn when we marched in the door to her. We struck up a bit of music for her and we danced on the floor. We danced around Beit in a circle. She started dancing herself inside the circle and that was an amazing sight to see Beit's hopping. She was short-winded when she stopped and had to sit down.

"By God, but you are tough lads," says she.

"Throw us a fist of money," said we, "because we would prefer that to any plámás."

In the Seabhac's story, that was the first of many visits paid by the young lads to the houses in their immediate locality in the course of an eventful and colourful day. And despite today's attractions of Christmas toys and television, groups of children still venture out with false faces, strange clothes and tin whistles, to collect money at the houses of the same locality on the Wren's Day.

In Ventry

In Dingle, as the night wore on, pubs emptied of one Wren only to be filled to the rafters by another. Small boys begged to be allowed to carry the heavy banner poles; small girls danced on corners; people of all ages alternately watched and joined or were dragged in.

A street was momentarily deserted: the night seemed to be waiting, the action was suspended. A dog sauntered in the gutter, forgetting in the sudden quiet his habitual furtiveness. Then, at a distance, the rattle of the drums and the penetrating notes of the fifes could be heard. Soon, the progress of the sound could be traced. It grew louder, swelled, seemed to reach over intervening houses to settle on the still abandoned street. At a corner the shape of the hobby horse emerged, a white form suspended in the air where it turned, its dark carrier at first merging with the darkness. Then the banner, held aloft, spanned the street as it negotiated the corner, borne by stocking-masked figures. And now the rabble, the followers on the pavements, costumed, masked figures, some linking arms,

Collecting in Cooleen

other cavorting and dancing, some weaving drunkenly with heads down, others jaunty, arms waving. The sound built, swirling around the tangle of buildings at the corner as the band entered the street. The silent stage of minutes earlier had become a sea swarming with bizarre images, the air thick with cacophony. Light and life had entered — raw and crude, energetic and raucous; a celebration, a festival, a shared drama. Details of the experience might be forgotten, the experience would not.

Two girls, arms linked in swirling dance, turned faster and faster. A woman strode along the street, arm in arm with a strawboy. A dark-clad figure with a false face of the Ayatollah Khomeini grabbed from behind a woman masked as a hag and wearing something like a jellaba and held her close; she reached her arms back, jabbed him sharply in the ribs, and he broke from her in a loping run down the street. A line of girls, arms round each others' necks, tried to march in step with the music.

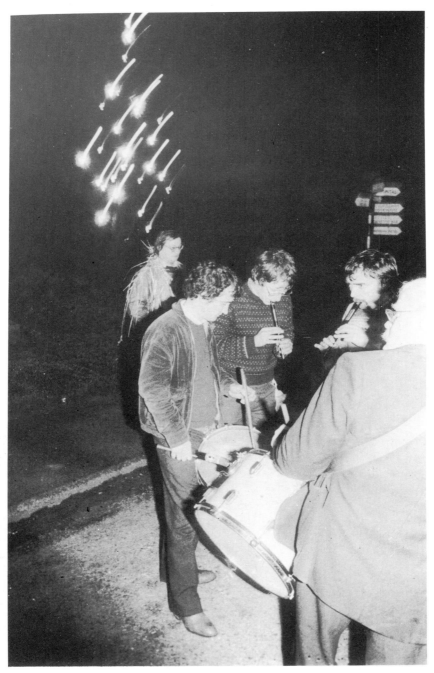

The final flourish under the Christmas tree

At the bottom of the street the Wren encountered another. The music of the fife and drum was suddenly competing with the amplified sound of accordion and drums. Children were grinning out from the back of the lorry on which the musicians were mounted. Someone waved a large tricolour in a crowd of people leaping in dance around the street. Amidst the confusion and hilarity, some emerged from pubs to stand outside the doors, drinks in hand; others dived inside. The limited order of the march was broken and the fife and drum band suddenly reduced to four standing on their own. Soon, all the pubs were full, the lorry had moved on and the street was quiet again but for the shouts and snatches of music from inside.

Musicians reappeared at irregular intervals onto the street, attracting varying crowds of followers; and it was not until after midnight that the Green and Gold made its last parade. Even then, Purdge, unsteadily supporting one of the banner poles, was still game for another round of the town as the musicians played their last tune under the lights of the Christmas tree.

The Wren was over for another year: an extraordinary day of extraordinary behaviour. In the days and weeks that followed it was generally agreed to have been one of the best Wren's days for many years.

To the outside observer the custom may seem an exotic survival, a strange vestige of pagan ceremony.

But it does not owe its continued observance to any notions of its antiquity. The fact that people have found it satisfying in the recent past is reason enough for its continuance. The numbers that have been involved over the years have varied, but it has always been a hard core of few people who have carried out the necessary preparations.

There are many in Dingle, both men and women, who have never marched on the Wren, and many who only participated as children. Some disapprove of it. A week after the Wren's day, one publican (who, ironically, had been an active Wrenboy in his youth) said:

> We lock the doors against them. They'd come in and you wouldn't know what they'd be taking. I can't vouch for this myself now, because I didn't see it, but I heard it alright from someone that did see it, that a crowd of them were in G------'s and they took the pint glasses with them away out of the place for their own ball night back in B------------- (a townland near Dingle). That was a disgrace. But the disgusting thing about the Wren's day over the years is that it introduced a lot of very young fellows to the drink for the first time. They'd be wearing masks and they'd be drinking away behind the masks and you wouldn't know who they were. Normally, of course, they wouldn't have been served at all. I've seen them there laid out on the ground at the end of the day, dead drunk.

It is not by accident that one speaks of the Wren*boys*, for it has been very much a male group activity. Both boys and girls may be frightened by the hobby horse or by the loud noise of the band or the animal masks and rigs, but girls run a particular danger of becoming upset by being manhandled. It can be disturbing for anyone, young or old, male or female, to find themselves being

pushed and shoved, prodded and poked by some antic apparition which calls them by name but which is itself anonymous behind a mask. And however jovial the intentions of the Wrenboys (and they are not always jovial — they are often excited and drunk) any woman or girl who is not self-confident and thick-skinnned can easily be upset. In recent years quite a number of women have participated, and most of these would give little credence to complaints of rough handling; but again, there are those who regret venturing out, and those who stay at home for the day.

For myself, as an observer who has come from outside to live in Dingle, it is both easy and difficult to understand the Wren: easy, in that it is so patently *there* — it requires no explanation, it simply *is*. Difficult, in that it expresses so many elements of the past and the present, all of which are closely related in a complex network or mosaic, that to isolate particular elements means to risk distortion. Its origins and history do have some bearing, but those who participate pay no homage to history: their dedication is to present enjoyment.

The Wren is drama which has not only dispensed with the proscenium arch, it has dispensed with the theatre. Indeed, it is a kind of drama which predates either structure. And in terms of the much-discussed relationship between audience and players, it is an event in which there is no such distinction. A drama of participation, then, and an expression of belonging to a people and a place.

It tells no story, contains no plot, does not explore character. There is no performance such as the mummers' play, no plotted action or dialogue. Yet there is action of a kind, which takes place in a set pattern, within which the actors choose their own roles from a stock of social and cultural reference. Rigs reflect two standard figures of European folk drama: the Fool and the Old Woman. There is movement, costume, masking and music. In the combination of these elements emotions may be evoked or evinced. It is an occasion full of ambiguity: a group of strawboys moving down the street, faces, identities hidden behind high conical headgear, can convey a sense of menace, of vague terror even; and this is not to say that they are not also just neighbours dressed up for the day, for the entertainment, for the crack. In the dark confines of night-time streets loud, insistent music of the fifes and drums fills the senses as the parade passes; then, of a sudden, an animal mask is thrust in the watcher's face and mocking laughter accompanies a dig in the ribs; and, as quickly as it came, the apparition is gone.

The Wren evokes images whose resonances touch chords of feeling, echoing in the viewers' minds. It may bring to the surface certain fears, but it does so that they may be rejected, for it is an affirmative experience; and if there is discord provoked by drunkenness, rowdy high spirits going over the top, this takes place within an overall dedication to unity. Through the rest of the year, people live their separate lives, but on the Wren's day the distances are suddenly foreshortened, everyone is engaged in the same act of enjoyment.

Such language will seem overblown to most who know the Wren: it is, after all, a fairly disorganised day of energetic fun which no one is at pains to analyse. Nevertheless, such language may go some way towards explaining why the tradition is still maintained.

Some of the elements which were important in the Wrens of fifty years ago have lapsed, yet the festival has not lost its vigour, and it is difficult to say what it is about the present-day Wren that is essential to its character and function. The September Wren festival in Listowel, organised as a competition, has little in common — despite its similar trappings — with the Dingle Wren. If the Dingle Wren were to become like Listowel, or if it were to become a tourist attraction, it would immediately lose its essence (and anyone reading this book might bear in mind that there is simply no point in going to observe a participatory event such as the Wren). And if attempts were made in Dingle to regiment or codify the events of the day its essence would be similarly lost. The Wren may be correctly regarded as a traditional folk custom, but tradition is not an element which is rigidly invoked as a static notion; as it operates in the preparations, tradition accomodates change and is no more nor less than a feeling on the part of the participants about what is right or appropriate.

If it had no current function, it would not survive; and its prime function is to provide enjoyment. And while other forms of enjoyment are available throughout the year, only the Wren offers such a shared experience; in doing so, it offers a release from the restrictions and tensions of the small-town society of Dingle. There can be a stifling, claustrophobic atmosphere for anyone growing up and living within the small community of the town (population about 1,500) and of the peninsula (about 5,000). Everyone knows, or seems to know, everyone else's business, and this effectively imposes many restraints and strains, which to some people can be a severe burden. This closeness can militate, too, against initiative and self-confidence, which have already been sapped by the emigration and poverty of previous generations. Thus, a day in the year when the constraints are relaxed and energetic celebration prevails makes a lot of sense.

A close-knit community does also have its virtues. There is an atmosphere as of an extended family, and at its best it fosters a network of mutual support. To the outsider an immediately striking feature is the sense of security that allows Dingle people to leave cars unlocked, keys in the doors of their homes, bicycles lying unpadlocked beside the road. And there is a deeper sense of security, too, which explains more than anything else why so many of the young people who leave return constantly for weekends; why so many who work as teachers, secretaries, labourers, nurses, far from their home town, retain a strong sense of identity with the place and, although they know that they cannot make their lives and work in Dingle, yet they yearn to be there. For the people of Dingle, whether at home or abroad, it is not just a place: it is a state of mind

and of being. For many growing up in it, it is a place to escape, it is a
condition rejected in favour of what is perceived as the more real
world of getting on, of career and prosperity, of maturity and
fulfilment. Yet it also exerts a compelling attraction even for those
who have struggled to leave it. Of all those alive today who were
born in Dingle, many more live elsewhere than live in the place
itself, and for many of the emigrants their most haunting image is of
the Wren.

The Wren would be nothing if it were not great fun. And it is a
source of anecdotes for winter nights long afterwards. Dingle people
can make a story out of tying their shoelaces, and the encounters
and events of the Wren provide a fund of conversational riches
which is readily exploited. It is in many ways a ramshackle affair: in
the sense that it is a performance, it is performed with no great skill,
and even where skill is shown it is not particularly important. But it
is richly entertaining and enjoyable, a roisterous day of carousing,
playfulness, music, parading and acting the fool.

Some days later the committee of the Green and Gold would
meet and do its sums. The collection had amounted to £246.50;
after expenses — for the Christmas tree and its lights, the big drum, a
new pelt for one of the small drums, for the oats and twine and other
small items — had been deducted, a cheque for £145 would go to St
Mary of the Angels residential special home for children in Beaufort.

On the morning after the night before, the streets were deserted.
A light, insistent rain fell from an overcast sky. Winter seemed to
have settled back into its grey routine. Outside Lynch's in Upper
Main Street the debris of straws still carpeted the pavement and
gutter, but birds no longer clustered there. In the alley beside
O'Flaherty's the body of the hobby horse rested on beer barrels
behind the wire mesh gates. At the corner of Green Street and Main
Street a battered signpost was decorated with remnants of a straw
suit.

91

Footnotes

1. Violet Alford, *The Hobby Horse and Other Animal Masks* London 1978; p. xiii
2. Venetia Newall, "Two English Fire Festivals in Relation to Their Contemporary Social Setting" *Western Folklore* Vol XXXI, No 4, October 1972; p. 245
3. Venetia Newall, "Up-Helly Aa: A Shetland Winter Festival" *Arv: Journal of Scandinavian Folklore* Vol 34, 1978; p. 42
4. Quoted in Newall, "Up-Helly Aa" p. 91
5. See Joseph P. O'Reilly, "On the 'Kerry Straw Cloak Exhibit'" *Proceedings of the Royal Irish Academy* Vol XXV, Section C, Nos 1-4, 1904
6. Giraldus Cambrensis, *Topographia Hibernica* (ed. O'Meara)
7. Newall, "Up-Helly Aa", p. 41
8. Ibid, p. 58
9. Newall, "Two English Fire Festivals", p. 245
10. Recorded from singing of John Joe Gleeson by the author, 1978